Anton Schulte

IS
LIFE
WORTH
LIVING?

Pickering & Inglis
LONDON — GLASGOW

Title of the German Original:
Anton Schulte "Lohnt es sich zu leben?"
TELOS-Sondertaschenbuch S 700
© Copyright 1976 by Brendow Verlag, D-4130 Moers 1

ISBN 0 7208 0423 X

Cat. No. 01/0909

First printing 1978

Printed in West Germany for PICKERING & INGLIS LTD, 26, Bothwell Street, Glasgow G2 6 PA.

Cover-Photo: laenderpress
Textfotos: dpa 9, 13, 15, 17, 18, 25, 35, 41, 45, 51, 53, 57, 63
Öffentliche Bausparkasse Wttbg. 7 – foto-present 11, 47 – Jim Roddy 21
Huber-Winter 23 – Windstosser 27 – Petri 28
Billy-Graham-Ass. 31 – Bruckmann 33 – Jim Roddy 39 – Autor 43
Licht im Osten 51 – EBA-Evang. Bild-Agentur 59, 61
Printed in West-Germany 1978

IS LIFE WORTH LIVING?

If some wealthy man declares that "Life is well worth living" we are scarcely surprised: money, we think, makes all wishes come true. If some young fellow, just accepted by the lovely girl of his choice, goes around muttering "Its good to be alive!" – that's what we might expect. People on the bright side of life do feel that living is infinitely worth while, and tend to broadcast their joy, even though the experience may prove shortlived and shallow.

I was twenty-three years old before I could say, with total conviction, that life is worth living. I was not wealthy, nor engaged to a lovely girl; I had won no lottery, nor fallen upon any good fortune. A senseless war had stolen my best years so far. Soldiering, and being a prisoner of war, I had found life so far a dead loss. To get free, I had contracted to work for a year on a Scottish farm. Overtime, at three shillings a row hoeing carrots, bought my first suit in a second-hand shop, when the war ended; my bicycle came from a scrap dealer, and I had to knock it into running order. Even so, I could still say life is worth living.

My home, and indeed my whole birthplace in the Ruhr, had been totally destroyed by an aerial mine. My father was killed in a bomb-attack in the last months of the war, and my brother is buried somewhere in Russian soil. I myself belonged to the cheated and duped war generation. All were reasons enough to be extremely miserable, and even to despair. Yet even then I was able to say,

"life is worth living".

"What sparks off love in our hearts?"

The couple pictured here might well be asking that, and not finding an answer. Those three crucial words, "I love you", hold a secret that no one really understands. So when a baby is born into the world, joy breaks through. We watch the child crawling, we listen eagerly to its first attempts at "Mama", we dote excitedly upon its first hesitating steps as it begins to learn to walk – and our own lives have a new fascination. The child, too, before it knows the difference between night and day, before it can count or sing, feels already how good life is, sheltered by others. The growing child senses that two people especially belong together, not simply being married but also understanding each other, and striving to please each other. Set within love, life is infinitely worth while.

Life is worth living too, in situations where illness (for example) prompts the caring hand, the comforting, encouraging word; where someone unemployed finds help readily offered; where a kind answer is given to unkind words; where even the old can say "I am not alone. I have not lived in vain."

Then life has purpose, and life is ever worth while if one understands the purpose with which the Creator invested life. When God planned and created man, it was that man should live in companionship with Him – not only in a life after death but also here and now. When God created all living things He created man too, and He said of life – "Behold, how good it is!"

And so it was, very good. But now?

In Britain alone, in 1976, 136,000 marriages were dissolved. Partners simply separated, though some had children. Certainly, during creation, God pronounced man good: but our daily papers are full of the most abominable things done by men – hatred and murder, theft, cheating, violence. What has happened to man, originally so good, to make him behave so badly now?

Those marriages, now broken, once began with fine intentions. The partners trusted each other, and looked with confidence to the future. They became one – "one flesh" – as God intended when He created them. But it did not last. Life for them did not fulfil its worthwhile plan.

Living together just did not work out – but the ones to suffer most are the children.

How can they possibly find life worth living? For that matter, how can anyone disappointed, despairing, over the inconsiderate behaviour of others say that life is worth while? Yet anyone – anyone at all – can reach this positive evaluation of life for himself. Anyone can experience a change so radical that he can come to accept his present position in life. But only if he is ready to face the reality of life, not fooling himself but realising frankly where the causes of disappointment and despair really lie.

A doctor seeks the cause of pain through diagnosis: not until that has been found can treatment and cure begin. So it is with the goal and essence of life itself. The Bible

tells of rebellion by the first people who were put into the garden of Eden, and how that later Cain killed his brother Abel. Since that fateful day conflict and war have never ceased.

We read in the daily press of one catastrophe after another. We have become accustomed to such headlines as, Hijacking, Kidnapping, and accounts of open war-like struggles between nations. Daily the situation seems to deteriorate. Who could have foreseen, a few years ago, that tension and violence would so take the upper hand? Yet the Bible does foretell that in the last days wars and rumours of war will increase, indeed we are already in the first stages of this "end time".

This frightening situation is consciously created, not only because the mass media of communication – radio, television, and the press – report quickly and world-wide the condition of our time, but because only bad news is considered worth reporting. We might even call it manipulation, when the bad, the negative, the evil events are so concentrated upon. But in reality there is not only a world of hate, murder, and war: there is another world, of goodness, and kindness, and peace. It is still possible to say, "life is worth living".

Can we talk of the beauty of life while confronted with a tank on Palestine's Golan Heights?

Tank-commander Chaim Itzak has a wife and children in Tel Aviv. When not serving as a soldier, he works with an orange-packing firm, carrying the name known

world-wide – Jaffa. Like most Israelis, he owns a house purchased for 300,000 (Isreali) pounds. He earns 2,500 (Israeli) pounds a month, and although he has two children he must pay 250 in taxes – probably the highest percentage in the world.

Chaim was only a child when his parents were abducted and driven, in a long freight car journey, to the German gas-chambers, where they died. It is a miracle that Chaim survived, he was taken into care by friends who hid him. In this way he was sheltered from the hatred which again and again confronted the descendants of Abrahan, Isaac, and Jacob.

Chaim's wife, who is dark-skinned, was born in Yemen. There, her parents were not permitted to walk on the road, simply because they were Jews. They had to use the paths beside the roads, provided for cattle. These are but two out of almost three million Jews who preferred to leave other countries of the world and to move into the land promised to their forefathers – to Abraham, Isaac, Jacob – by God Himself.

Is life worth the living to people driven from their homes and families by such ill-usage?

The United Nations sends troops, but has no solution at hand.

East and West seek to keep their fingers out of Israel, because they are afraid. To the Arab peoples, Israel appears an intruder because for almost 2,000 years (since the expulsion of the Jews from Judea by the Romans in the year AD 130) Arabs had lived there until the

foundation of independent Israel in 1948. Israel herself considers this new foundation but a return to the land which is rightfully theirs, where they as a nation wish to live in freedom and in peace. The Bible had already predicted, thousands of years ago, this conflict between the Arabs and Israel. The Bible also says that the swords will become ploughshares, and there will be peace.

But this has not happened yet. The Israeli soldier sits on his tank und reads his Bible – not an unusual sight in Israel. It happens more often now, as a result of deeper thinking. For since the war of Yom Kippur the young people of Israel have grasped this truth: their origin and their destiny are written in the Bible.

At the University of Jerusalem, professors and students alike use the biblical records as a basis for their studies and research. They have rediscovered old irrigation systems from the times of Solomon, and retraced old cites missing for thousands of years. Scrolls, too, have been discovered which now prove that the Bible is in fact an ancient book in which are written God's thoughts about the future: therefore, the Israelis feel, their own future is in the Bible. But it contains not only the future of Israel, only, but the future of the world – God's future for mankind.

What, therefore, most concerns any individual, what makes the greatest difference to him, is in the end religion.

At this point, when we think of the world's future and our own, the question is inevitably raised about the

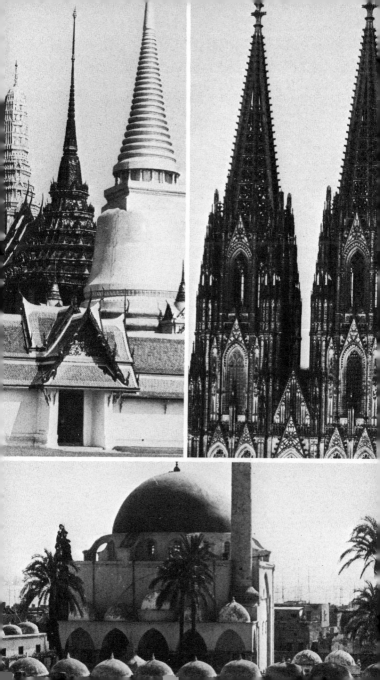

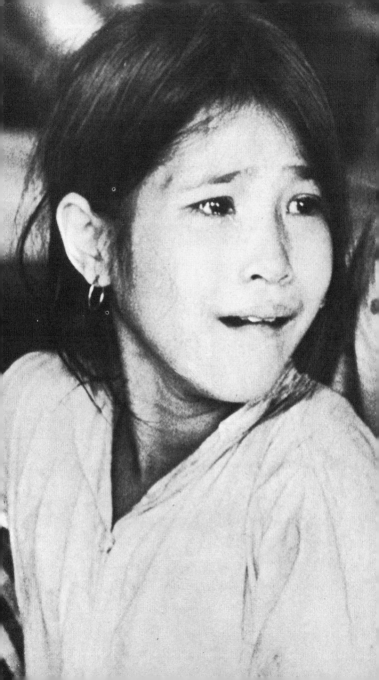

origin of the powers and forces at work in the world. If I know where I come from, I know also where I am going; if I know who has created me, I know also for whom I am intended. But at this present time the only religion mankind is experiencing is that of fear.

The film producers, concentrating upon one catastrophic tragedy after another, make their fortunes out of this widespread fear, but their raw material is provided by real events. For, while it is known that earthquakes rise in number every century, the last few years have seen a dramatic increase – eleven major 'quakes costing two million lives this century. The Bible names this as one feature of the End. We can surely see for ourselves how far the hands have moved on the world-clock!

In face of such facts, one might suppose that only dreamers and sadists could still declare life to be worth living – unless there is some other perspective, unless it is possible to look at life from some different angle, and assess its value by some other standard.

In preparation for a Church Conference-Day, a vote was taken upon what will dominate the mind of Federal Germany. The majority replied,

"Anxiety – an anxious dread". But Jesus said: "In the world you will have tribulation, but be of good cheer, I have overcome the world" (John 16:33).

We can, then, be free, of this fearful dread of life, through Jesus Christ, who overcame the world. In

19

situations of danger it is normal to be afraid, a purely natural reaction. But one can become dominated by fear, crippled and tormented by anxiety, and find no escape. Such inner dread can grow, and grip the soul. Desperate for self-deliverance, he longs to break out of this enveloping mood, to tear off the strait-jacket of fear. Frantically he tries this way and that, but all his struggles are panic-stricken, and futile.

"See, buy, and be happy"

These three words adorned an advertisement outside a large department store in a pedestrian precinct where we were holding an open-air service. They gave me the introduction to my message! Could it really be true, that one sees, buys, and is automatically content, and happy? Occasionally it may be so. But we cannot buy everything we see, and sometimes we are not happy with what we buy. Sometimes, too, the happiness does not last as long as the payments. Still, many people do indeed seek distraction from life's realities in an orgy of spending, hoping no doubt to change themselves by a lavish expenditure on things.

Some people, certainly, consume ridiculous amounts of food, either thoughtlessly, or to help them face awkward situations. Sometimes the idleness of holiday, at other times the strain of examinations, encourages such over-eating. Worry, or sorrow, can actually increase our weight! Yet others, though careful of their figures and their food, are just as extravagant over luxuries: an ordinary car is not good enough; their holiday must be expensive; their clothes, not practical

and suitable but always "way out" and better than their neighbour's. All this is symptomatic of an underlying fear lest they miss out on something worth while in life: as though things we can make, or things we can buy, could ever fulfil the deepest longings of the soul.

For many, again, in these days, drugs are the chosen avenue of escape from the dread anxiety of life. The deepest cause is usually emotional stress. Ask many addicts the reason for their dilemma, and you will generally be told of –

1. Lack of love – not feeling accepted by others, not being understood by family or friends, great loneliness, deep disappointment;

2. A desire to die, to break finally from an intolerable situation; the drug offers forgetfulness, or at least the opportunity to be someone different for a few hours;

3. Seeking for God.

Again and again, drug addicts in acute distress admit their longing for some overwhelming religious experience –

– and this is true also, basically, of many who misuse alcohol.

The cause, very often, can be traced backwards into childhood, to a lack of affection in the home, to conflicts of opinion between the parents, and disagreements on how to bring up the children. A child is sometimes afraid of quarrels, and of punishment; and is gi-

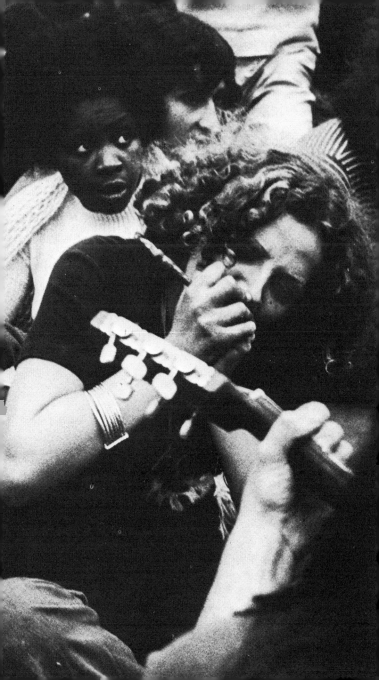

ven no chance to speak up, or to be listened to in the family, or even among friends. Yet those who, in consequence, look for comfort in drugs or in alcohol soon find that these offer no solution. The victims merely get further astray, hoodwink themselves, and once sober again taste all the more bitter disappointment. Even adults need affection, security, love, no less than young people: and a totally satisfying religious experience can in truth be found – but not in drugs!

An Arab student deliberately jumped to his death past the fireman who sought to save him.

Not every rash outburst – 'I am going to end it all' – is to be taken seriously; but for all that, nearly as many commit suicide each year as are killed on the roads, and this does not include unsuccessful attempts at self-destruction. And all too often, those intent on suicide take others with them into death, sometimes a husband, or a wife, or children.

Behind all this lies the same inward, anxious dread. A business man gives up the constant struggle against defeat; a mother cannot bear the shame of her own child's failure; a wife feels unable to endure the way her husband degrades her – there is a long list of the reasons that have driven people to suicide. One day a colleague of mine heard a voice on the telephone declare, "I am quitting – now! And taking my children with me." At first, she thought the man was intoxicated, and did not believe him. She asked to speak to the children, and was shocked to hear a little one say, "We are going to heaven with Daddy now. Its really nice there."

Mercifully, we were able to prevent the worst happening.

But is anything really changed by ending this life? We shall remain, before God, just what we are here, on earth: the good does not become evil, through death, nor the evil good. Suicide solves nothing; it is an attempt to escape from one's living self, which is impossible. "Ending it all" does not achieve a life worth while! What is really needed is a new beginning. And a new beginning is possible, but only through is forgiveness. It is through forgiveness that we come into fellowship with God, in this life – not through death.

Think it through once more. Man as God created him was "very good". God Himself thought so – wer are not here taking an artist's high opinion of his own paintings where the customers think differently! No, it is the assessment of God himself, who created all things, who at the same time decided what was good and evil, who gave to every creature a purpose, who is the supreme Judge of men, and also King over His own creation: –

"And God saw everything that He had made, and behold it was very good." (Genesis 1:31)

Yet those who observe what is happening around them must be driven at some time to the final conclusion that man is fundamentally evil. He not only cannot love, and be helpful, and trust; he positively hates, and murders, and destroys at an increasing rate. Moving rapidly towards a suicidal goal, man is fast destroying himself and his planet. What has happened to him?

Why does this man, so good in the beginning, now behave so badly?

We find the explanation in the Bible. There it is recorded that man was in fellowship with God, and was to remain in this fellowship, but his so remaining depended upon man's own free will. God did not desire a puppet theatre, with marionettes dancing as He pulled the strings. Man had to decide for himself, whether to obey God or not to obey Him. There was no apple tree in Paradise, as some believed when they were children, but a very special tree which enabled man to recognise what was good, what evil. God forbade man to eat from this tree, but tempted by Satan – from whom all evil originated – man rebelled against God's will. By violating God's commandment, man experienced spiritual death separation from God. And the consequences were catastrophic. Man's intended destiny was fellowship with God through voluntary obedience: he deviated from this goal when he broke God's commandment. The Bible calls this "sin". The consequence was, that man for the first time experienced what evil, and guilt, and a nagging, pestilent conscience, really are. So man tried to hide from God – which impossible. Subsequently Cain killed his brother Abel, and Cain's way of thinking has dominated the world ever since.

Jealousy, hatred, revenge, and war.

Out of such bitter experience, fashioned by man for himself, grows a deep religious longing. Man lost fel-

lowship with God in Paradise; since then, all have lived in separation from God. Violating God's law, we no longer enjoy fellowship with Him: but we do long for it. And because we can find forgiveness of sin, this longing can be fulfilled.

God is willing to forgive, and the destroyed relationship with Him can be restored. This happens even among men: the moment we honestly forgive each other, all anxious dread of each other, vanishes; our enemies become our friends.

Arms that once brandished fists now are linked in a reconciling embrace; where there is forgiveness of sin, there peace makes its way into the human heart.

Mankind has known, ever since the Fall from God, that it needs someone to come to its aid. Men called him "Saviour", and longed for his coming. God said in the beginning that He would send salvation; it would be of some help simply to trust in God's promise and await the Saviour.

Emperors and conquerors of various kinds took advantage of man's longing for salvation, and called themselves "saviours". One Roman emperor had a coin minted with the inscription, "The Emperor Augustus, Saviour of the World". And so, to this day, would-be leaders, and other ideologists, have advertised themselves as "bringing salvation". Others have, again and again, devised their own schemes for salvation, through religious endeavours, or man-made philosophies. But all such human efforts yield no true solutions.

The Bible says, "When the time had fully come, God sent forth his Son." God became man, in the person of Christ, passing from eternity into time. Before earth was created, God had prepared this plan so that man could receive forgiveness of sins. But God did not carry out His plan, to send His Son as Saviour for all men, until the right time, until men realised they could not help themselves.

So Jesus Christ, the Son of God, entered this world. He is man's only chance – his God-given chance. This is why He says, "I am the way". He is not merely one guide among many, or one of several possible ways of salvation: He is the only way to God. For He alone is without sin, and He alone died on the cross at Calvary for our sins.

What actually happened on that cross, at Calvary? A man died, one who according to His own testimony, and according to what many others said of Him, is God's Son. This was confirmed, not only by His words, but by His deeds. And a sign was fastened to the cross, naming the accusation against Jesus, written in the three languages most used at that time, Hebrew, Latin and Greek: it read, "Jesus from Nazareth, King of the Jews."

Jesus Christ was treated, and was ultimately put to death, as a common criminal.

Christ did not die for His own sin: not even His enemies found any guilt in Him. One who was not guilty suffered for those who were; the one Son of God for all

mankind. As the Bible says, "For our sake He made Him to be sin who knew no sin, so that in Him we might become the righteousness of God." (2. Corinthians 5:21) When Christ died on the cross He bore the sins of all people, of all times, all our fault, and all our guilt. As He said from the cross "It is finished." Divine forgiveness was now available for every man. When we read that He has made us "righteous" it means simply that our sin has been removed from us to bring us back into a "right" relationship with God. For every man who accepts Christ's death as substitution for his own, it becomes as though he had never sinned. So the Bible says that God "will remember their sin no more". Thus, with no possibility of our deserving it, we were given salvation, when Jesus Christ took our sins upon himself on the cross at Calvary. As we read in Romans 3:23–24, "... since all have sinned and fall short of the glory of God, they are justified by His grace as a gift, through the redemption which is in Christ Jesus." The longing to be righteous, to act righteously, to experience righteousness in return, has stirred within man throughout the centuries. All the laws, the processes of law, the law-courts of the world confirm this. Yet –

If righteousness be applied without reconciliation, the result may be harsh, even brutal.

For example, imagine the following situation: two people who had wronged each other stood before a judge, each insisting he was not guilty. The judge uncovered the truth, and through his verdict righteousness was achieved. That should have made everything fine, each man receiving his just desert. But righteousness is

only one part: in fact, the two went their ways as enemies, because no reconciliation took place.

Not only did Jesus Christ make us righteous before God, He also reconciled us with the holy God who had good cause to be angry with us. Such reconciliation puts everything right: the sin is forgiven, the enmity too between God and man is taken away.

There is no more fighting, no bitterness, there are no grudges, no revenge; instead, where there is reconciliation, there is joy.

If a man will not accept this justification through Jesus Christ, and will not be reconciled through Him who died on the cross for us all, he stays as he was, separated from God, an enemy of God through sin. He remains on the "broad way" which the Bible says leads to destruction. Though we cannot picture heaven and hell – for we can imagine only things of time and space, whereas heaven and hell reach far beyond time and space – but we do know that God has described heaven as the most beautiful place, hell as the most dreadful. In any case, it is far less important to know what heaven looks like, than to be sure we will enter there!

If a prisoner is under long sentence, his only hope lies in mercy. If he is ever to be pardoned, it will not be because he never broke the law, nor because the judge made a mistake, but through the compassionate gift of mercy. Likewise the forgiveness of sins through Jesus Christ is a gift of divine mercy – the greatest gift ever given: but it has to be accepted, too, as every other gift must be. This calls for a personal decision. It matters nothing how great our sin, how old we are, what race or what church we belong to: everyone must personally accept this gift of forgiveness through the salvation made possible by Jesus Christ.

God first accepts us. He did so even when we broke His commandments. Though it grieved God that we went astray, He had to accept our decision. In the same way, He accepts our decision to break away from sin and become obedient. Just as the thought of sin precedes the committing of it, so the obedience of faith begins with a mental decision, a decision that leads to willingness, and so to action. So every man can now come to God through Jesus Christ and say, "I am sorry I sinned, O God; I want now to obey; I want now to leave my old way of life and be obedient to your will."

I made my personal decision for Jesus Christ while still a war-prisoner, towards the end of the war.

During the war I found myself in Italy, in spite of all danger still alive. Life dragged on – I was prisoner on a ship on the ocean, a lumberjack in America, hungry and without hope in Belgium. From here I was transported with many others to Scotland, where I slowly gained my freedom, step by step.

After that, I tried hard to make up for everything life had not given me, but it was impossible. What I thought would be a means of joy vanished in my hands. I appeared as a jolly and happy man, especially among friends, but I did not feel happy. In my heart I was searching for an inner peace; actually, I had been looking for it for many years.

In the prisoner-of-war camp I had had much time to read. I studied the different philosophies of life, but the more I read the more hopeless it all seemed to me. I told myself there *must* be something in life to make it worth while.

At this time I still thought of myself as an atheist. I denied the existence of God. But I was not sure. The questions, "Where did everything come from?" and "How did the process of life begin?" would not leave me in peace, but brought me back, again and again, to the question about God.

It was there in Scotland, after I received my freedom, that some Christians invited me to come to a "get-together". A few young men there talked about their life, saying that God was alive, and had sent His son, who died for our sins on Golgotha. They said that this Jesus Christ had been raised again. He was alive, and had set their lives in order.

All this was said in such a simple, sincere and yet convincing way that I was very impressed. I attended repeatedly the Saturday evening meetings, and heard the Gospel of Jesus Christ in this exceptional manner.

Then came the evening which brought the decisive change in my life. In a neighbouring village, in the hall

of an evangelical church, there was a similar meeting. Again some young people talked about their life, and especially about the changes that Jesus Christ had wrought in them. I knew, very definitely, that what these young people had, and what they were talking about, was exactly what I was longing for, fellowship with God, forgiveness of my sins, renewal of my whole thinking and behaviour.

That evening, after the meeting ended, I did not just go home but took the opportunity to talk with one of these men. He opened his Bible and showed me by means of God's Word that before God I was a sinner and had done evil. He asked me whether I was preapared to break with my sin. I suddenly saw how bound and fettered I was in my life. **I knew for certain: I cannot go on like this, if I want to have God in my life, and follow His ways.**

That evening, I gave my life consciously to Jesus Christ, to receive forgiveness from Him and to start a new life by His strength. Then I went home, outwardly the same Anton Schulte that I had been before, but inwardly something quite new had come to be.

After being released from the prisoner-of-war camp, like so many others I returned to my bombed homeland. **I drove through the Ruhr in a street-car:** to my right and left along the road, in some parts of the town, only ruins remained. Much of the rubble was cleared, temporarily, to the sides of the road, though some streets were still blocked. I stood at the spot where once had been

the house in which I was born. I walked through the graveyard, searching for my father's grave. Yet I can honestly say that inspite of all that I had lost, I had peace within my heart. I knew that I had a heavenly Father, God Himself, who knew my life, and held it in His hands.

It was difficult to find a place to live. I found a job in Düsseldorf, but I had to share a room with ten other men. This experience of over-crowding, and very limited space, caused me much depression, but I found myself able to endure it. Indeed, my life was filled with a joy that astounded those around me. That which gave my life fulfilment was not bound up with the things one can buy, or make. Eating, drinking, clothes, home, were all part of my life but they did not constitute my life. There were greater, more significant things in life for me. Life, to me, was having peace with God, and with other people. It was having the strength to think positively, a strength which only grows from faith.

Before this time I never knew what the resurrection of Jesus Christ really meant.

It seemed to be mere phantasy, without meaning for me personally. After I had become obedient in my heart to Jesus Christ, I noticed, all of a sudden, that I received a strength I had never experienced before. This followed several temptations, that sometimes ended in failure. I learned now to withstand the temptations, and found I could say "No" to sin, and had the strength to break with it. Over and over again I was able to do something good, that before had seemed impossible. I was able to

resolve quarrels, to apologise, to clear up misunderstandings. Did I have a stronger will now, or was I morally better? Yes, but not in my own strength. From day to day I learned increasingly to trust in Jesus Christ – who is alive today. He did not remain in the tomb: He lives, now, within me; and in His power I can do things I could never manage on my own.

So I am a Christian, I told myself. Because I consciously said "Yes" to Jesus Christ, I wanted also to live a life worthy of Christ. Back then, along, with other Christians, we visited refugees in bunkers, basements, large warehouses, where hundreds, even thousands, lived in confined places, to bring them some relief. I had no great plan to improve the world, but I felt my own responsibility to help others, spiritually and materially, beside continuing my daily job. During this time I learned that life is much more than mere food and clothes and a place to live. One can be content with what one has – with a contentment that comes from not despairing in difficult situations but, instead, by personally accepting them. Yet this must not be confused with a mere optimistic pat on the back. This ability to accept difficulties is possible because Christ has accepted us – and provided we have accepted Him as well.

Things have changed a lot in Germany since then, but it became very clear to me that the essentials in life are more than income, and growth in the economy.

I was talking with an Ashanti chief in Africa about the problems of the nations of the Third World. This man,

who made his decision for Christ during his student days as a result of the work of the YMCA in London, was very thankful for Federal Germany's financial help in Ghana. He hoped that Ghana would receive yet more help from the wealthier nations,

but he added that this would not be the final solution. The people must be freed from superstition, which can be achieved only as a result of a spiritual revival – the deliverance that he had experienced, and that everyone who accepts Jesus Christ as his personal Saviour and Lord can also experience.

On the other hand, while in Japan I also realised that even a highly developed country, with the most modern technology and management, capital and education, cannot buy that deliverance from the fear of spirits. Indeed, modern superstitions in countries sharing western civilisation are only new versions of old fears, the deep dread of all-pervading fate.

So I had learned that even where one does not expect joy, even where life is beset with pain and tears, one can still find security in God through faith in Jesus Christ. For example –

I have stood at the bedside of many sick people.

Christians react differently to pain and suffering, but the more one has learned to trust the Lord in good days, the stronger this trust will be in days of suffering. A visit I once paid to a sick person in the Sauerland impressed me deeply.

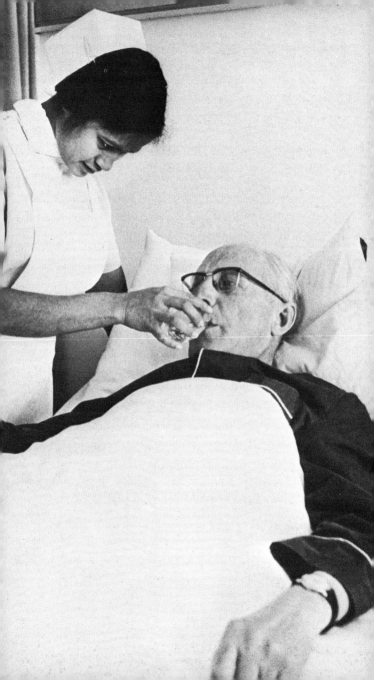

A sick man, perhaps seventy years old, lay before me, having been paralysed for seven years, and now incapable of dressing himself. I had been speaking, during the evenings, at one of the local churches, and he sent a message asking me to visit him. His voice was only a whisper, but he very joyfully told me how he had experienced forgiveness, and reconciliation with God. I thought I was expected to bring comfort to a sick brother; instead, it was I who was strengthened through his testimony. He had no complaints about his sorry condition. In a matter-of-fact way he spoke about his illness, and very touchingly he talked about the nearness of God, and of his experience of receiving a strength which the Spirit of God giving us in the particular way that our personal need requires.

Just so does the Bible record God's promise: "As thy days, so will thy strength be."

Even that sick saint could not answer all the questions one would ask about suffering, and illness, and what is the meaning in it all, but inspite of his illness he found much to be grateful for. He gave thanks to God, and to those around him, and in this attitude found his own fulfilment.

I am not sure that I could react so well if I were ill. At the moment it would seem incredible if I could: bust since that visit I know what God can do in one's life.

During a stay in London, I visited the Tower not just to see the Crown jewels, for the queue waiting to get in the first time I was there was far too long! I was interested in the dungeons, hollowed out of the solid rock, in which noble prisoners were locked away

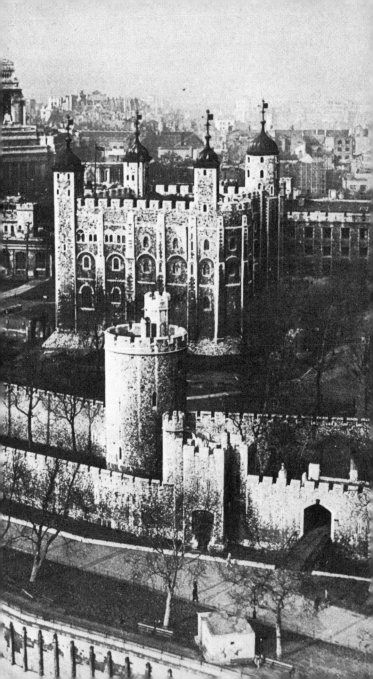

weeks, even months, before their execution. I wanted to see what many of those who had been imprisoned because of their faith had written while waiting for death. The very first line my eye fell upon read: "The more suffering, the more glory." Added to this was the apostle Paul's testimony, taken from his letter to the Romans (8:18): "I consider that the sufferings of this present time are not worth comparing with the glory that is to be revealed to us."

This gives us part of an answer to the question regarding the meaning of suffering. It also gives us a standard by which we can measure a fulfilled life. It is a life in which the goal lies beyond physical death: the Bible calls it "eternal life". Only with this goal in mind can one say, even amidst all the troubles, chaos, suffering and misery in this world, that life is worth living, because our life on earth is only a "passing through" to the true life in the presence of God. When we know of the goal which we are "living towards", when we know salvation from the broad way leading to destruction, and when we realise that we have been purchased for an eternal fellowship with God – then we may receive strength which can change us completely.

Today, in most areas of the world, the persecution of Christians continues, in some form or other.

Jesus did not promise us a life without suffering, pain, contempt, or persecution: through the apostle Paul He has urged us to be ready to suffer: "Take your share of suffering as a good soldier of Christ Jesus." (2. Timothy 2:3) This suffering with Christ does not always mean physical persecution.

A woman returning from Siberia told how a small group of Christians baptised their new converts in the river swollen by melting snows. A young gire sent by the secret service to observe this said to her superior, "If you send me to that place once again, I will become an Christian too; there is something about these people that I just cannot explain!"

This certain "something" is eternal life. Eternal life does not begin at death: it is God's own life: it always was, and for ever it will be. Everyone who has fellowship with God through Jesus Christ receives it – for we not only have forgiveness of sin through Jesus Christ, but also eternal life, which never ends.

Hence the apostle Paul can say "If God is for us, who is against us? He who did not spare His own Son, but gave Him up for us all, will He not also give us all things with Him?" (Romans 8:31, 32). The Bible also provides the answer to this question: "Nothing shall separate us from the love of God . . ."

There is the truth: God loves us. It means that He cares for each of us so personally that He helps us, and has prepared an eternal home for us. I know that I am going there, and will be welcome to enter, because God has so promised, as it is written in 1. John 5:12,13: "He who hast the Son has life, he who has not the Son of God has not life. We know we have it because it is so written in scripture. And Jesus assures us: My word will never pass away.

A rubbish bin and a petrol station are necessities in the everyday life of modern man.

He can dispose of all the rubbish he no longer needs in the rubbish bin, and he drives to the petrol station every time he needs fuel to journey on.

We may liken prayer both to the bin and to the petrol pump. In prayer we unload all that worries us, and does not truly belong in our lives. We can tell God of such things, entrust them to Him, and let Him take care of everything.

When first we begin our life with Jesus we do not always realise how many unnecessary burdens we carry around; later, we recognise these burdens to be hindrances in our new way of life. Old ways of thinking, of reacting, of behaving – all this can now be brought before the Lord as sin, in our prayers. The prophet of the Old Testament uses an apt description: "He has buried our sin where the sea is deepest"; for the sea is the largest dumping-ground there is! This makes crystal clear that no matter what we "unload" before Jesus, none of it will ever be used against us. That is why the Bible says, "God will never think about their transgressions again."

But prayer not only unloads all the rubbish of sin: it is also our spiritual petrol pump where we receive new strength from God, in order to avoid transgressions and obey Christ in every way.

When we buy a machine it is usually accompanied by directions for use, which can be very important. Every time my wife an I purchase some new appliance for the home, my wife says, "read the instructions before you break something!" She has every right to speak so, for once already I have done just that!

But our lives are much more complicated than any machine. Only He who has created life can fully understand it – God Himself. He knows "what it takes", how we must behave, if our life is to function properly.

God's "practical instructions for life" are – the Bible.

The Bible states what God had placed in the human heart in the beginning, but what, from generation to generation, because of the faithless behaviour of men, has faded and been forgotten. Therefore God sent His messengers, such as Moses, who brought God's commandments down from Sinai; and later the prophets, who shared with us the thoughts of God. This is how the Bible originated, and why we so frequently read, "Thus saith the Lord." David, who shared God's thoughts with us mainly in song, and who with God's help rose from being a shepherd boy to the status of king tells us in Psalm 119:105: "The word is a lamp to my feet and a light to my path."

In modern English, it might read "my flashlight . . . and a strettlamp all the way home." So, if we read the Bible and apply what we read in our lives, we see clearly, our way is illuminated, we detect hindrances and dangers, and will surely reach our goal.

"Think before you act", we often say: – fine advice, if only we always did just that! And my new life, too, must first be thought through. I belong to God, I have made Jesus Lord of my life. Now, I wish also to know what He, to whom I have given my life, expects of me. This I can learn from the Bible. In it I can find what God wants me to do. He has given me His cousel, instruction, and commandments; and the Bible says, "Peace is with those who love your law. They will not stumble." If I do not want to stumble and fall, I must make up my mind to do God's will.

The process is plain: first clarify mentally – say – the whole issue of private property, and decide that you will not steal: then you can leave other people's possessions alone. The decision reached in the mind is the secret of obedience.

Those not familiar with Christian life fear they may still not be able to do what they have decided is right. But we have no reason to be afraid. For one who becomes obedient to God receives the power of the Holy Spirit to carry out what he has obediently decided in his heart. Therefore the apostle Peter says, "And we are witnesses to these things, and so is the Holy Spirit whom God has given to those who obey him" (Acts 5:32). The Holy Spirit is God – and therefore the greatest power there is. Jesus said, "My grace is sufficient for you, for my strength is made perfect in weakness."

So, it is not our strength that is all-important, but our obedience: that permits the power of God to work within us.

Just as we must be born, physically, into a family, with father, mother, and perhaps brothers and sisters, so God does not place us in this world, in spiritual birth, as orphans, but gives us a spiritual family. All who believe in Jesus Christ belong together. A expression of this belonging together is found in the life of God's church.

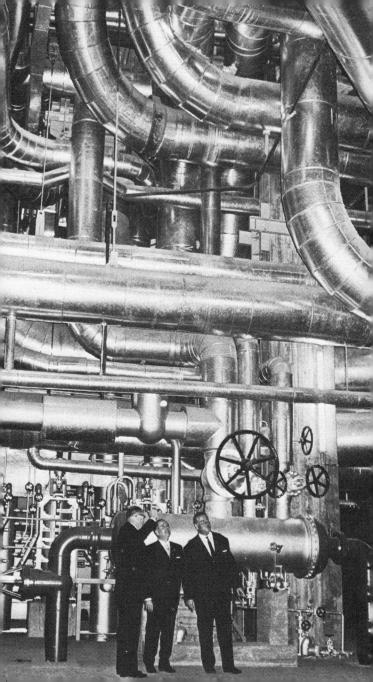

Such sharing in life does not develop automatically. I must be in fellowship with my brothers and sisters of my own free will.

Jesus promised that where two or three are gathered in His name, He will be in their midst. To live as the church of God does not mean that crowds of people have to be gathered together. Indeed, one can in practice apply what belongs to the everyday life of a family of God very much better if the group is small, and when we read the Bible together, we can exchange thoughts, discuss what we read and we experience stimulating fellowship with others. In order to cultivate this fellowship and help each other, we need personal contact with a church or a youth-group. The first Christian church had in addition to their large gatherings and assemblies, opportunities for spiritual orientation for new convert, **throught the practice of baptism and commuion, in small group.** They gathered for large meetings, but also had the breaking of bread in their homes (Acts 2:46).

All living things are composed of many tiny cells. Therefore the tiny cell is significant even in the church, and it is important that every Christian finds his place within one.

"You are the salt of the earth." In His sermon on the mount Jesus Christ made it very plain that we as Christians have a specific function in this world — that of salt. Salt is essentially different from the meat which it preserves. Salt has this characteristic, it penetrates into things and prevents them from becoming spoiled. In

this sense we as Christians are to be "the salt of the earth" – which means, we are to work within this world.

The measure in which we receive this power to be salt depends upon our personal contact with Jesus Christ, on the extent of our Bible-reading, on the time we spend in prayer, and on how obedient we are. It is a power which works both within us and through us. Wherever we are, be it in school, in the factory, at the office, or in the family circle, our influence may prevent evil being done, or at least may decrease its effect. Through our presence, and through our actions, we are like bastions against the influence of sin and evil in the world around us. That is why, trusting in this commission given to us by Jesus Christ, we are able to face our everyday life courageously.

For – let us not doubt it – as Christians in this world we have very special instructions from God:

God wants His ambassadors to represent Him, in all nations, all levels of society, all professions and trades.

We are to penetrate all of humanity with our mission. Jesus says, we are in the world but not of the world: that saying means that in proportion was we keep fellowship with Jesus Christ, and keep contact with His church – we will have a purifying effect in the world.

"Light of the world" we are called, too. A lighthouse shows sailors their way into the harbour; a car's headlights illumine the whole street at night; and –

Landing lights direct aircraft safely to the runway.

Where there is light one can see what is happening and this quality of illumination is given to all who follow Him.

So Jesus Christ describes Himself as the light of the world (John 8:12): Jesus says, "Whosoever follows me shall not walk in darkness but shall have the light of life." That is why He says, in the sermon on the mount, concerning those who follow Him, "You are the light of the world." (Matthew 5:14)

In other words, as Jesus Christ is Himself the light of the world, so everyone who has accepted Him will also become, through Him, a light in the world – provided we always remember that Jesus himself is our power to shine. The more we trust in Him, the more He can work in uns, and through us. Moreover, in His light, we who are Christians can look towards the future with hope, because the future is in God's hands. As we study the Bible, many things are made clear which help us to look beyond the difficulties, needs, and unanswered questions of the present. For the life we live now is not significant in itself: it is only a time of preparation for – God's new world.

So, inspite of all that is bad around us, the evil done in the world, the unanswered questions and the stress of these days, this is my personal experience, and the conviction it has brought me – that

LIFE IS WORTH LIVING.

If this book has raised questions in your mind, and you would like further help you can write to Anton Schulte at any of the following addresses:

GERMANY:

NEUES LEBEN
Postfach 13 80
D-5230 Altenkirchen/Ww.

WEST-GERMANY

GREAT BRITAIN:

NEW LIFE
Central Arcade
115/117 High Street
Ayr, Ayrshire
SCOTLAND

U.S.A.:

NEW LIFE
P.O. Box 929
Racine, Wisconsin
53405
U.S.A.

CANADA:

NEW LIFE
Box 8
White Rock,
B.C.
CANADA

The following literature is also available from these addresses:

"NEW LIFE REPORT" . . . a quarterly illustrated news report of the ministry of Anton Schulte and his team, sent free on request.

"QUIET TIME". . . . . . . quarterly Bible Study notes prepared by Anton Schulte, with a suggested Bible reading and brief comments. It is a valuable help for those seeking an aid to their private devotions. Sent free on request.

"THE GOODMOOD
FAMILY" . . . . a little booklet of children's stories written by Anton Schulte.